Troll Teacher Time Savers

Here's to Spring & Summer!

Reproducible Activity Sheets for Grades K-1

Troll Associates

Troll Teacher Time Savers provide a quick source of self-contained lessons and practice material, designed to be used as full-scale lessons or to make productive use of those precious extra minutes that sometimes turn up in the day's schedule.

Troll Teacher Time Savers can help you to prepare a made-to-order program for your students. Select the sequence of Time Savers that will meet your students' needs, and make as many photocopies of each page as you require. Since Time Savers include progressive levels of complexity and difficulty in each book, it is possible to individualize instruction, matching the needs of each student.

Those who need extra practice and reinforcement for catching up in their skills can benefit from Troll Teacher Time Savers, while other students can use Time Savers for enrichment or as a refresher for skills in which they haven't had recent practice. Time Savers can also be used to diagnose a student's knowledge and skills level, in order to see where extra practice is needed.

Time Savers can be used as homework assignments, classroom or small-group activities, shared learning with partners, or practice for standardized testing. See "Answer Key & Skills Index" to find the specific skill featured in each activity.

ANSWER KEY & SKILLS INDEX

Page 1, **My Monthly Calendar: (small-motor coordination)**

Page 2, **Spring Months: (small-motor coordination)**

Page 3, **March: (small-motor coordination)**

Page 4, **Peanut Fun: (letter recognition)**

Page 5, **Spring Is Here: (spelling)**

Page 6, **The Way to Freedom: (maze)**

Page 7, **St. Patrick's Day Surprise: (letter recognition)**

Page 8, **St. Patrick's Day Puzzler: (word recognition)**

Page 9, **Count & Color: (counting)**

Page 10, **Find the Shamrocks: (visual acuity)**

Page 11, **A Rainy Day: (counting)**

Page 12, **Rainbow Surprise: (colors)**

Page 13, **First Day of Spring: (word recognition)**

Page 14, **Time for Little Ducks: (counting)**

Page 15, **Spring Basket: (counting & colors)**

Page 16, **April: (small-motor coordination)**

Page 17, **April Fools': (colors)**

Page 18, **Foolish Fun: (true-false sentence analysis)**

Page 19, **Spring Flowers: (same/different)**

Page 20, **Hooray for Spring: (counting)**

Page 21, **Play Time: (sequencing)**

Page 22, **Barnyard Rhyme Time: (rhyming words)**

Page 23, **Things That Go Together: (same/different)**

```
I B R U L W S
K E A S T E R
A S B I U G U
M O B F D G W
C H I C K Q Y
P K T M O T E
```

```
X S U M M E R G
F B N S W I M S
U E F L A G H A
V A C A T I O N
I C G I E L T D
A H B E R S G C
```

```
A N M G O A L U Z C F
C E Z U J N J V B D I
L T W C K M K I C K E
B A L L B O O Q P M L
J S C O R E B T S R D
```

My Monthly Calendar

Name _____

paste month here

Sunday	Monday	Tuesday	Wednesday	Thursday	Friday	Saturday

Spring Months

PASTE
HERE

PASTE
HERE

PASTE
HERE

 CUT HERE

MARCH

APRIL

MAY

Color, cut
and glue
into the
right box.

Name_____ **Date** _____

2

March

My Name

Paste-Ins

CUT AND GLUE THESE
PICTURES IN THE RIGHT
SPOTS ON YOUR CALENDAR

FLOWERS

FLOWERS

SUNNY

SUNNY

SUNNY

CLOUDY

CLOUDY

CLOUDY

CLOUDY

SUNNY

SUNNY

SUNNY

SUNNY

SUNNY

SUNNY

ST. PATRICK'S DAY

SPRING BEGINS

PALM SUNDAY

WINDY

WINDY

WINDY

WINDY

WINDY

A GREAT DAY

A GREAT DAY

A GREAT DAY

A GREAT DAY

FULL MOON

JONQUIL

HAPPY BIRTHDAY!

HAPPY BIRTHDAY!

HAPPY BIRTHDAY!

KITE

KITE

RAIN

RAIN

RAIN

RAIN

RAIN

SNOW

SNOW

3

Peanut Fun

March is National Peanut Month. Color all the letters of the alphabet that you can find in the peanut.

Make a list of foods made from peanuts.

_____

_____

_____

_____

_____

_____

_____

_____

Name_____ **Date** _____

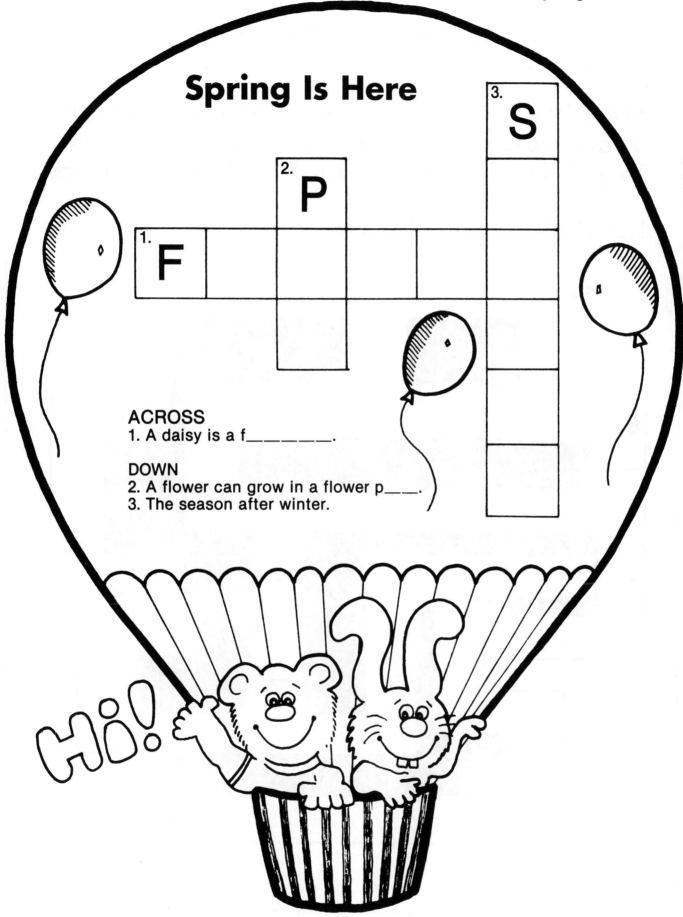

Spring Is Here

ACROSS
1. A daisy is a f_____.

DOWN
2. A flower can grow in a flower p___.
3. The season after winter.

Hi!

Name_____ Date _____

The Way to Freedom

March 10 is Harriet Tubman Day. Harriet Tubman was born a slave. She escaped and helped other slaves to escape too. The path they followed was called the Underground Railroad.

Help Harriet Tubman bring slaves to freedom.

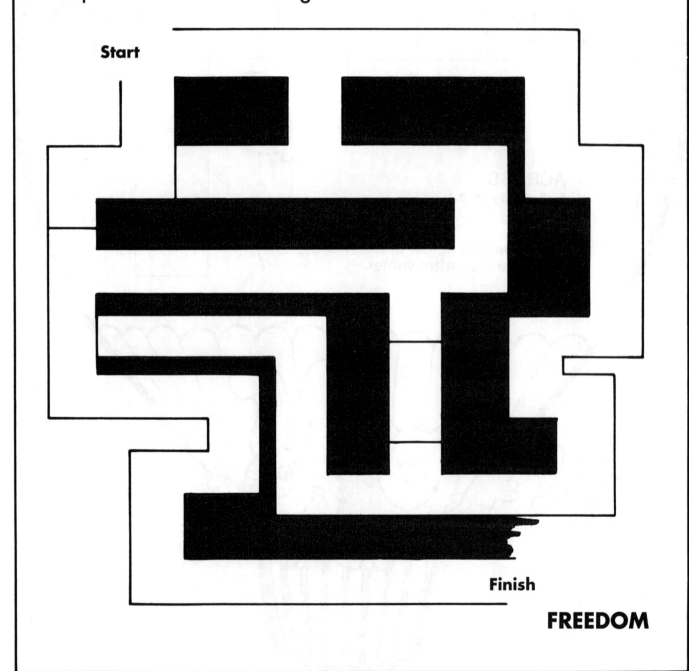

Start

Finish

FREEDOM

Name_____   Date _____

6

St. Patrick's Day Surprise

Color spaces marked with the letters.
You will have a

Name _____

Date _____

St. Patrick's Day Puzzler

G	F	S	M	G	L	R	S	A	U
O	A	E	A	R	U	K	H	C	T
L	E	P	R	E	C	H	A	U	N
D	G	I	T	E	K	D	M	N	O
A	X	H	K	N	D	Z	R	L	Y
T	J	N	S	C	R	E	O	J	Q
B	I	R	I	S	H	F	C	X	K
Y	Z	I	O	F	U	N	K	W	G

St. Patrick's Day is March 17th.
Find each of these 7 words in the puzzle
and circle it. Look across and down.
One is done for you.

LEPRECHAUN
GREEN
LUCK
SHAMROCK
IRISH
GOLD
FUN

Name_____   Date _____

8

Count & Color

How many hats?

Count all the hats on these leprechauns. How many are there? Color them green.

Name_____ Date _____

9

 # Find the Shamrocks

How many shamrocks can you find?

_____

Color them green.

Name_____ Date _____

A Rainy Day

Help Miguel count the raindrops. Write the numbers from 1-10 on the raindrops.

Name_____ Date_____

Rainbow Surprise

Read the color words in the flowers and on the rainbow.
Use your crayons to color the picture.

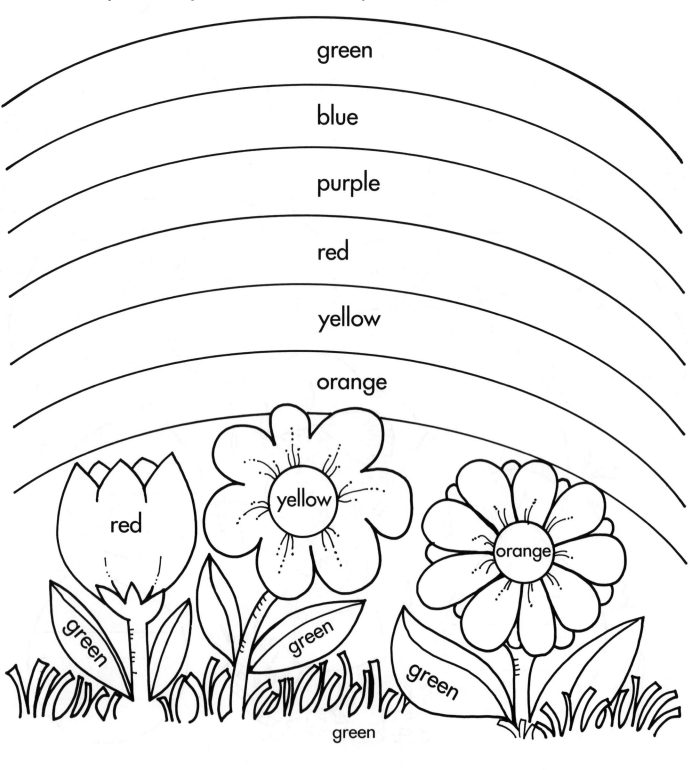

green

blue

purple

red

yellow

orange

red

yellow

orange

green

green

green

green

Name_____ **Date** _____

12

 # First Day of Spring

The first day of spring is usually March 20th or 21st. Here is a spring puzzle for you to do. Find each of these 7 words in the puzzle and circle it. Look across and down. One is done for you.

F	P	R	B	O	S
L	N	T	I	F	P
O	W	A	R	M	R
W	I	N	D	Y	I
E	G	G	S	L	N
R	B	E	E	S	G

BEES
FLOWER
WINDY
WARM
SPRING
BIRDS
EGGS

Name_____ Date_____

13

Time for Little Ducks

How many ducks are in the pond?

_____

Color them yellow.

How many are not in the pond?

_____

Color them orange.

Name_____   **Date** _____

14

Spring Basket

How many stripes
are on the basket? _____

Color the stripes
yellow and purple.
Color the chick yellow
and the hat blue.

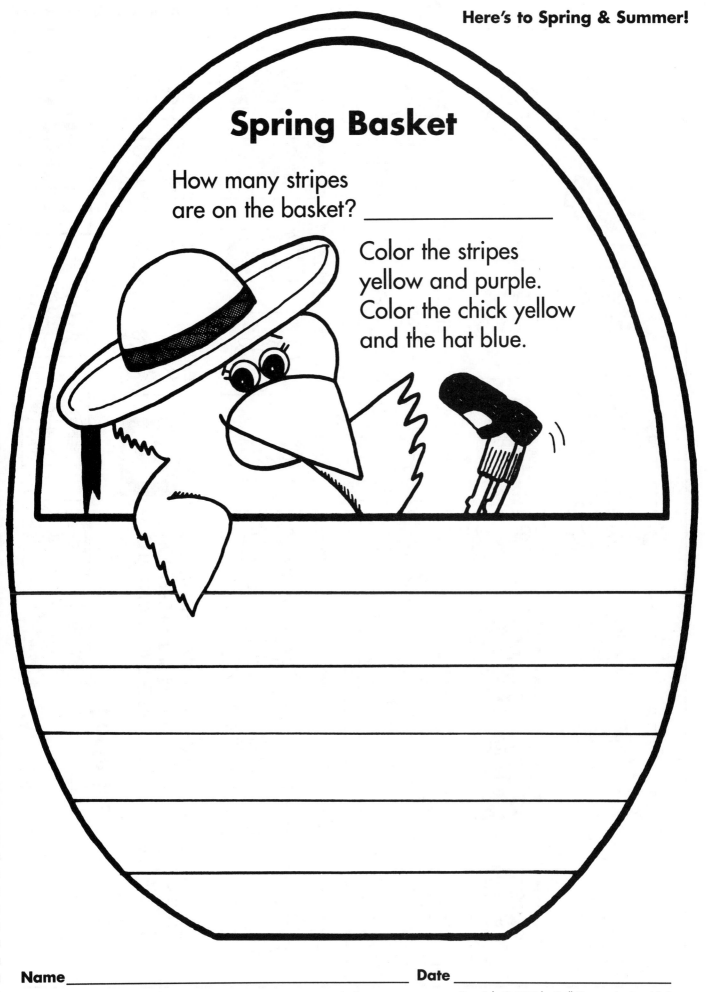

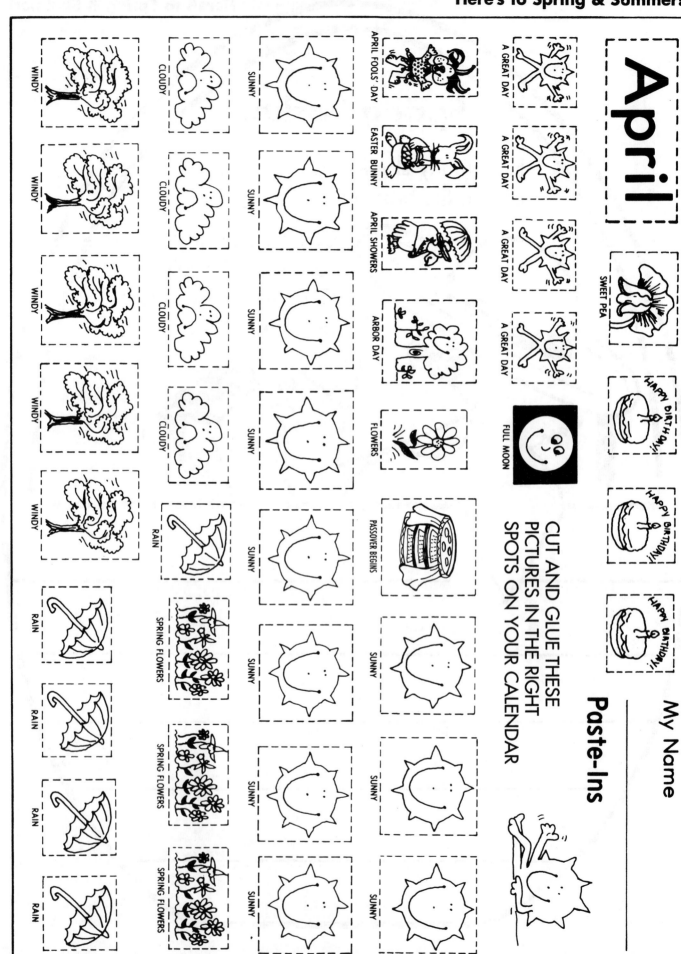

April

My Name _____

Paste-Ins

CUT AND GLUE THESE
PICTURES IN THE RIGHT
SPOTS ON YOUR CALENDAR

SWEET PEA

HAPPY BIRTHDAY!

HAPPY BIRTHDAY!

HAPPY BIRTHDAY!

A GREAT DAY
A GREAT DAY
A GREAT DAY
A GREAT DAY

APRIL FOOLS' DAY
EASTER BUNNY
APRIL SHOWERS
ARBOR DAY

FULL MOON
FLOWERS
PASSOVER BEGINS

SUNNY
SUNNY
SUNNY
SUNNY
SUNNY
SUNNY
SUNNY
SUNNY
SUNNY
SUNNY
SUNNY

CLOUDY
CLOUDY
CLOUDY
CLOUDY

SPRING FLOWERS
SPRING FLOWERS
SPRING FLOWERS
RAIN

WINDY
WINDY
WINDY
WINDY
WINDY

RAIN
RAIN
RAIN
RAIN

April Fools'

April Fools' Day is April 1st. We play silly jokes and do silly things. Color this silly-looking creature.

Foolish Fun

You never know what to believe on April Fools' Day. Below, circle what you know really isn't true. Then color the pictures.

Tee hee!

Birds fly.

Dogs dance.

Pigs shop.

Elephants are big.

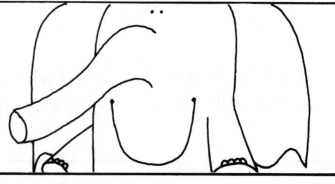

Name_____   Date _____

18

Spring Flowers

Color the flowers that are the same in each row.

Hooray for Spring

How many things are there in each row?
Write the number at the end of each row.
Then color the pictures.

Name_____   Date _____

Play Time

Put an X on the picture that doesn't belong.

Name_____ Date _____

Barnyard Rhyme Time

Put the animals into the barn. Cut out the animal words and glue them next to the words they rhyme with.

pen [   ]   boat [   ]

wig [   ]   box [   ]

house [   ]   stick [   ]

leap [   ]   luck [   ]

hen	fox	duck	pig
chick	goat	sheep	mouse

Name_____   **Date** _____

22

Things That Go Together

Circle what does not belong in each row.

Name_____

Date _____

Leap Frog

Help the frogs leap to their lily pads. Draw a line from the frog with the number word to the lily pad with its number.

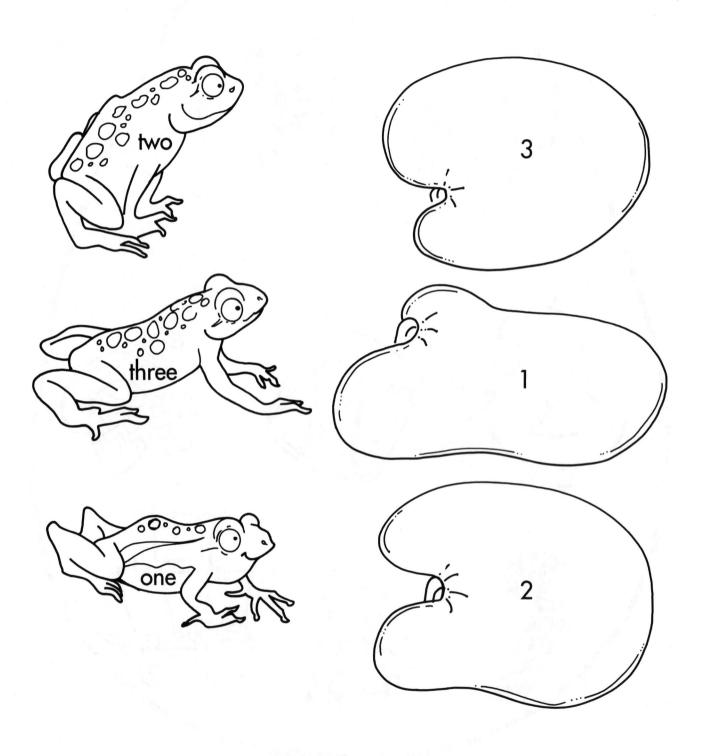

Hidden Letters

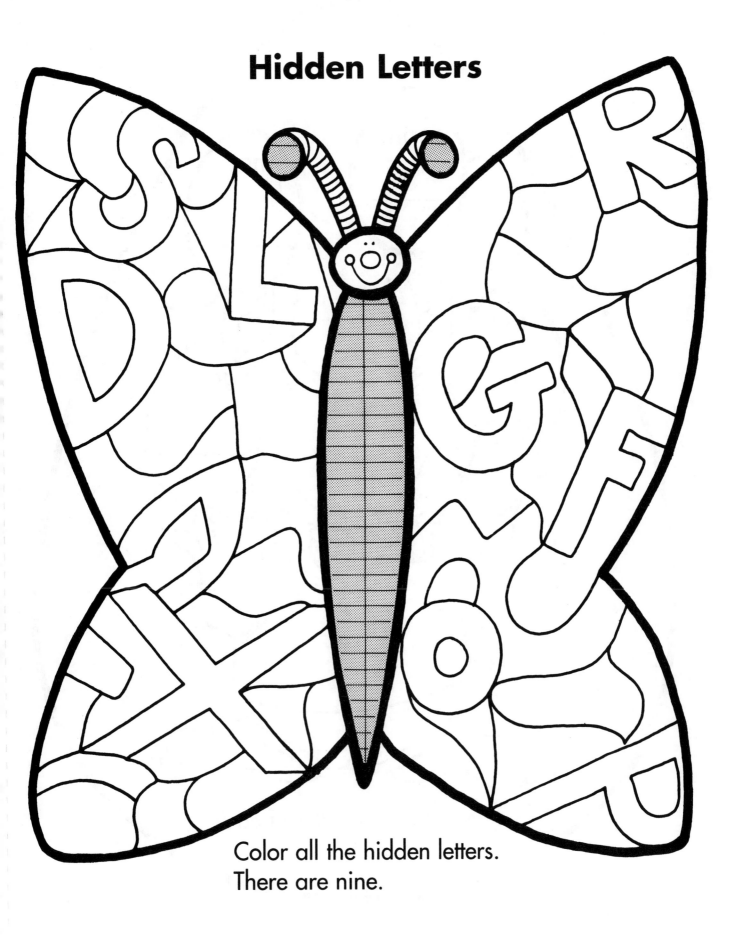

Color all the hidden letters.
There are nine.

Bunny Juggler

spring

hat

fun

grass

Write the first letter of each word on the line.

Name_____

Date _____

 # Eastertime

Count the eggs.
Write the answer
in the box.

Color the Easter
Bunny painting
the eggs.

Draw a Bunny

Draw what is
missing on
this bunny
and color it.

Name_____

Date _____

Surprise in the Basket

Connect the dots below to
see what is in the basket.

There are four

_____ _____ _____ _____

in the basket.

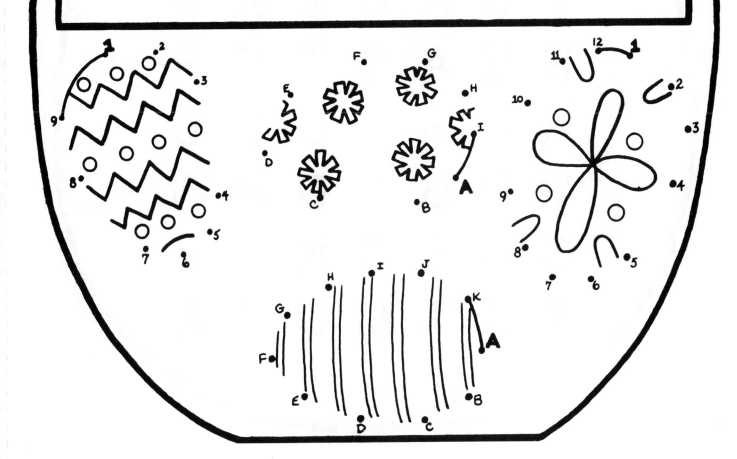

Name_____

Date_____

Easter Egg Hunt

Find these words below
and circle them.

EASTER   RABBIT

CHICK   EGG

I B R U L W S

K E A S T E R R

A S B I U G U

M O B F D G W

C H I C K Q Y

P K T M O T E

Easter Puzzle

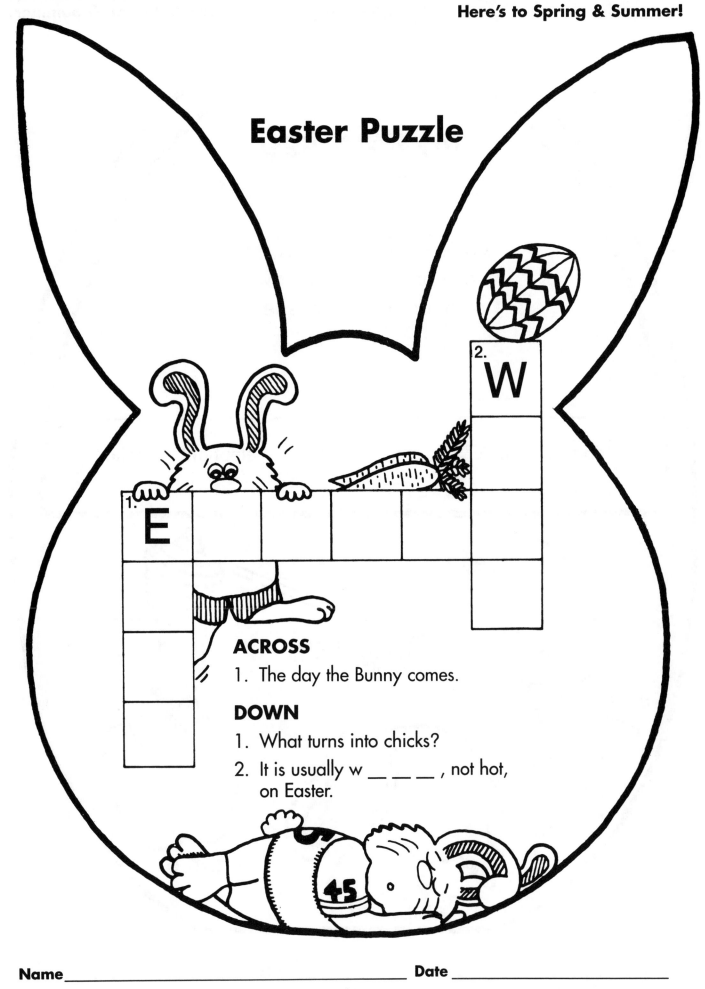

ACROSS

1. The day the Bunny comes.

DOWN

1. What turns into chicks?

2. It is usually w _ _ _ , not hot, on Easter.

Name_____ **Date**_____

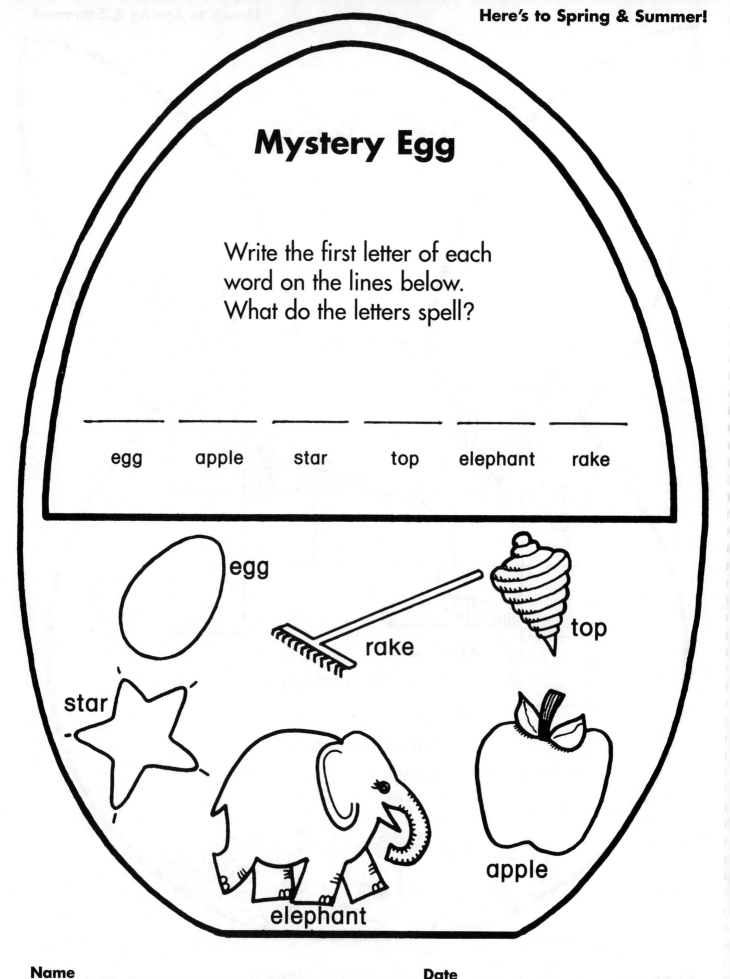

Mystery Egg

Write the first letter of each
word on the lines below.
What do the letters spell?

____ ____ ____ ____ ____ ____

egg   apple   star   top   elephant   rake

egg

rake

top

star

apple

elephant

Name_____ Date_____

⬭⬭⬬ Egg Holders ⬬⬭⬭

Color animals and strips.
Cut out and glue strips on construction paper.
Cut out animals.
Tape ends of strips where shown.
Tape one animal to back of
each base.
Place an egg in each holder.

CUT HERE

TAPE

CUT HERE

TAPE

CUT HERE

TAPE

CUT HERE

Picnic Pals

José and Gabrielle want to go on a spring picnic. They don't know what to take because their directions are all mixed up. Can you help them? Cut out the sentences. Then glue them in the picnic basket in the correct order.

Then, put in drinks.

First, add the sandwiches.

Finally, have a picnic!

Next, pack some fruit.

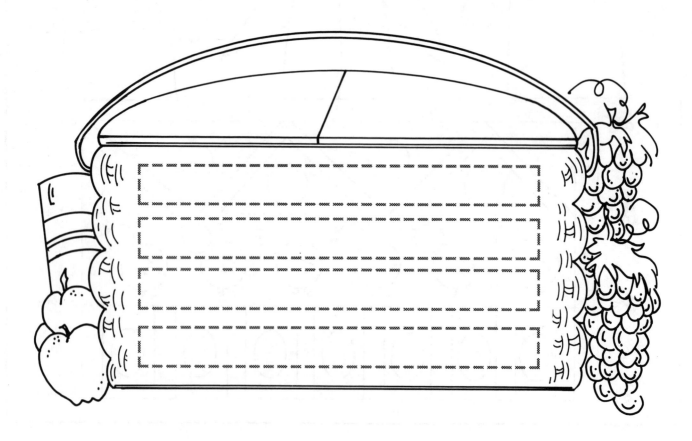

Name_____ Date _____

A Special Plate

The seder is a Passover feast. "Seder" means order, and the seder follows a certain order. In the center of the table is the seder plate. There are six foods on the seder plate: a bone, an egg, parsley, a mixture of chopped apples and nuts, and two bitter foods, such as horseradish and onion.

Color the foods on the bottom. Then cut them out and glue them to the plate.

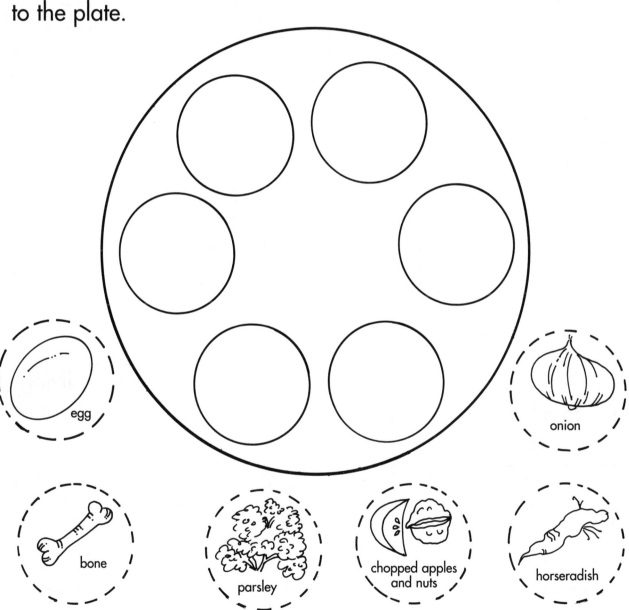

egg

onion

bone

parsley

chopped apples
and nuts

horseradish

Name_____ **Date** _____

35

Find the Matzah

Matzah is a special Passover food.
Whoever finds the hidden matzah wins a prize.
Help Jason and Abby find the matzah in the living room.

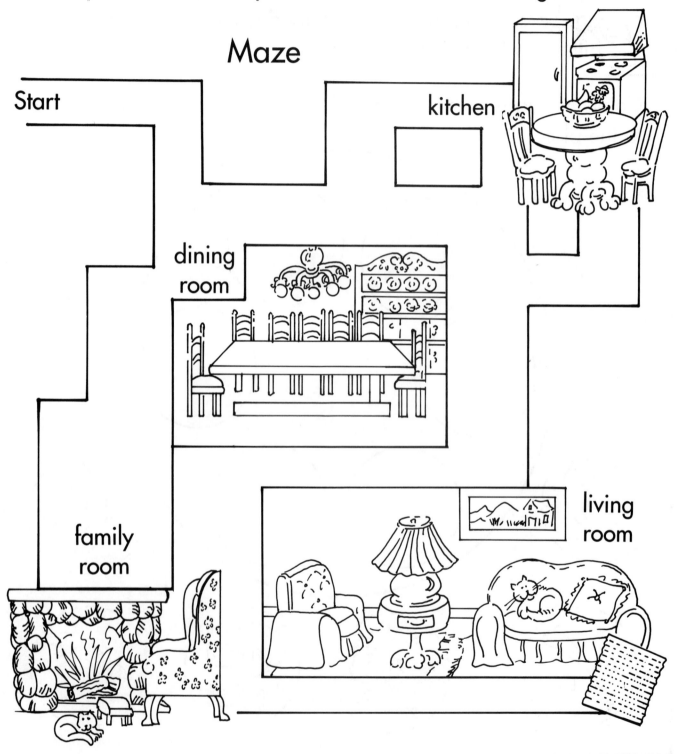

Maze

Start

kitchen

dining
room

living
room

family
room

Name_____

Date_____

What Comes Next?

 On Arbor Day we plant trees.
Did you ever plant a seed?
Circle the number under each
picture to show what
happened 1st, 2nd, 3rd, and 4th.

1 2 3 4

1 2 3 4

1 2 3 4

1 2 3 4

Name_____ **Date**_____

37

Butterfly Rhymes

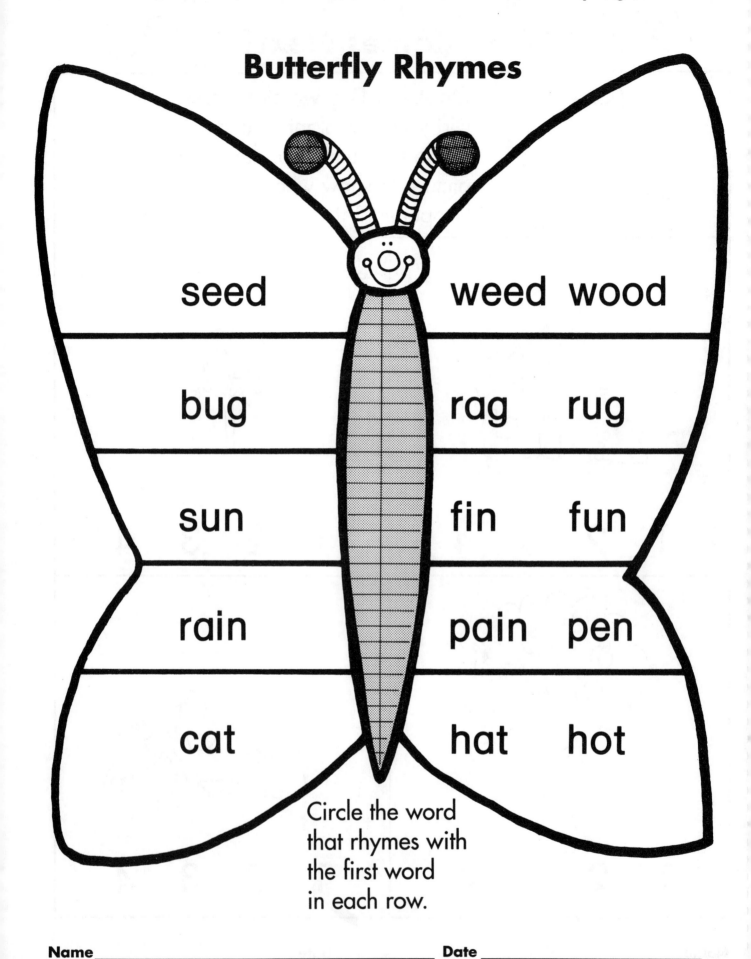

seed	weed	wood
bug	rag	rug
sun	fin	fun
rain	pain	pen
cat	hat	hot

Circle the word that rhymes with the first word in each row.

Name _____ Date _____

Wiggly Words

This worm has mixed up his words.
Can you unscramble the letters?

__ __ __
n s u

__ __ __ __
d i b r

__ __ __
e b e

Name_____ Date _____

39

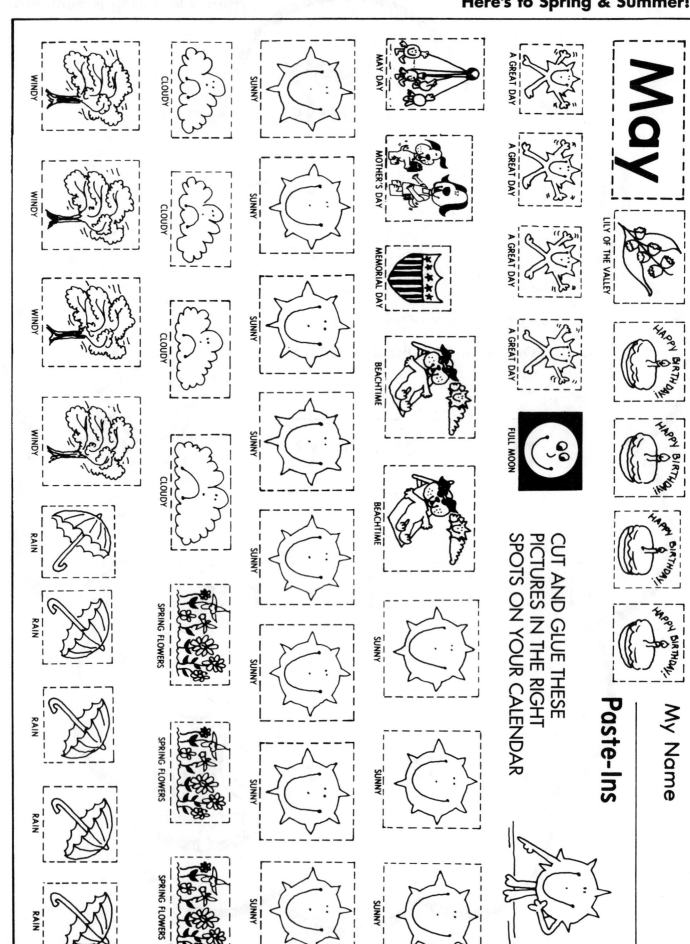

May

My Name

Paste-Ins

CUT AND GLUE THESE
PICTURES IN THE RIGHT
SPOTS ON YOUR CALENDAR

LILY OF THE VALLEY

FULL MOON

A GREAT DAY

A GREAT DAY

A GREAT DAY

A GREAT DAY

HAPPY BIRTHDAY!

HAPPY BIRTHDAY!

HAPPY BIRTHDAY!

HAPPY BIRTHDAY!

MAY DAY

MOTHER'S DAY

MEMORIAL DAY

BEACHTIME

BEACHTIME

SUNNY

SUNNY

SUNNY

SUNNY

SUNNY

SUNNY

SUNNY

SUNNY

SUNNY

CLOUDY

CLOUDY

CLOUDY

CLOUDY

WINDY

WINDY

WINDY

WINDY

RAIN

RAIN

RAIN

RAIN

SPRING FLOWERS

SPRING FLOWERS

SPRING FLOWERS

🌸 May Day Flowers 🌸

May Day, May 1st, is the celebration of flowers. Below are different flowers. See if you can say their names. Color them. Then draw and color your own flower in the empty space.

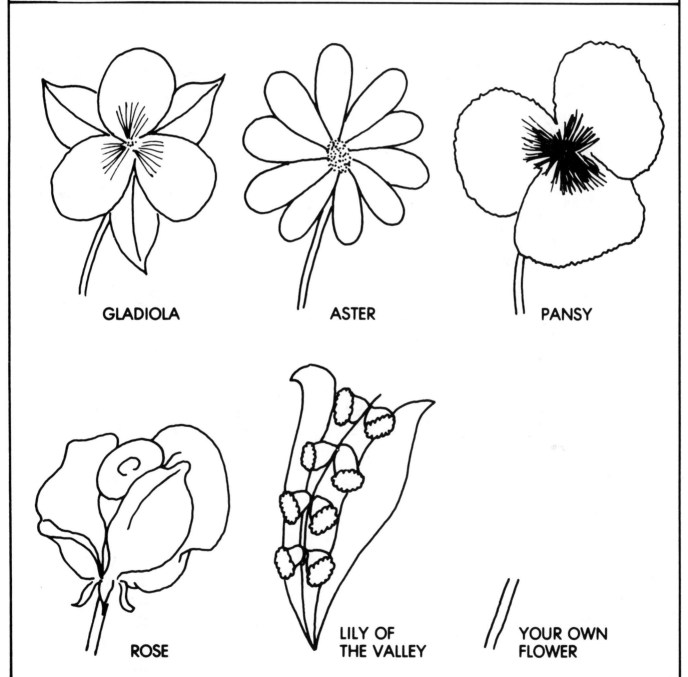

GLADIOLA

ASTER

PANSY

ROSE

LILY OF THE VALLEY

YOUR OWN FLOWER

Name_____ Date _____

Sunflower Power

Read the center of each sunflower. Cut, then glue, the correct petals to its sunflower.

school

beach

swim

teacher

flag

water

pail

crayons

chalk

sea

sand

paper

Name_____ **Date**_____

42

🌼 Mother's Day Card 🌼

Mother's Day is the second Sunday in May.
Here is a card you can make.

Cut out
on dotted
line.

Color card.
Fold in half.

Happy Mother's
Day

Love,
Mary

Sign your
name inside!

Happy Mother's
Day

Name _____ **Date** _____

43

To Someone
Special,

I LOVE YOU!

HAPPY MOTHER'S DAY

LOVE,

Color the spring flowers and sign your name below.

Mother's Day Planter

1. Color flower shapes and cut them out.

2. Glue one flower shape to a pipe cleaner or straw.

3. Glue the other to it, back-to-back.

4. Color 2 leaves green. Cut them out.

5. Attach to pipe cleaner or straw.

6. Make the other 3 flowers.

7. Make 4 holes in a styrofoam block.

8. Place your 4 flowers in it. You now have a flower planter for Mom!

Name_____ **Date** _____

Baseball Maze

Help this bunny find his baseball.

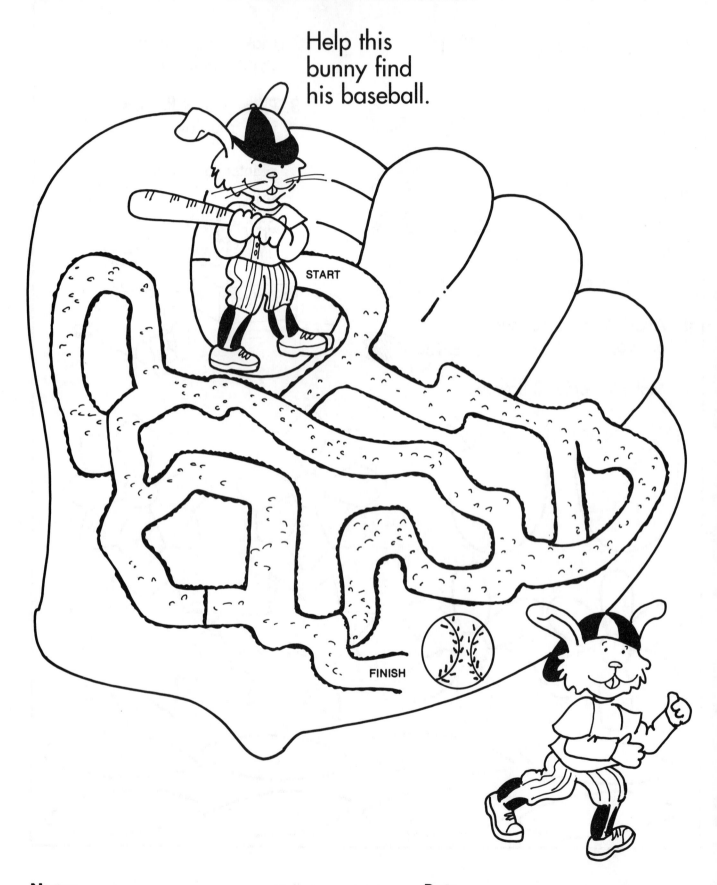

START

FINISH

Name_____ Date_____

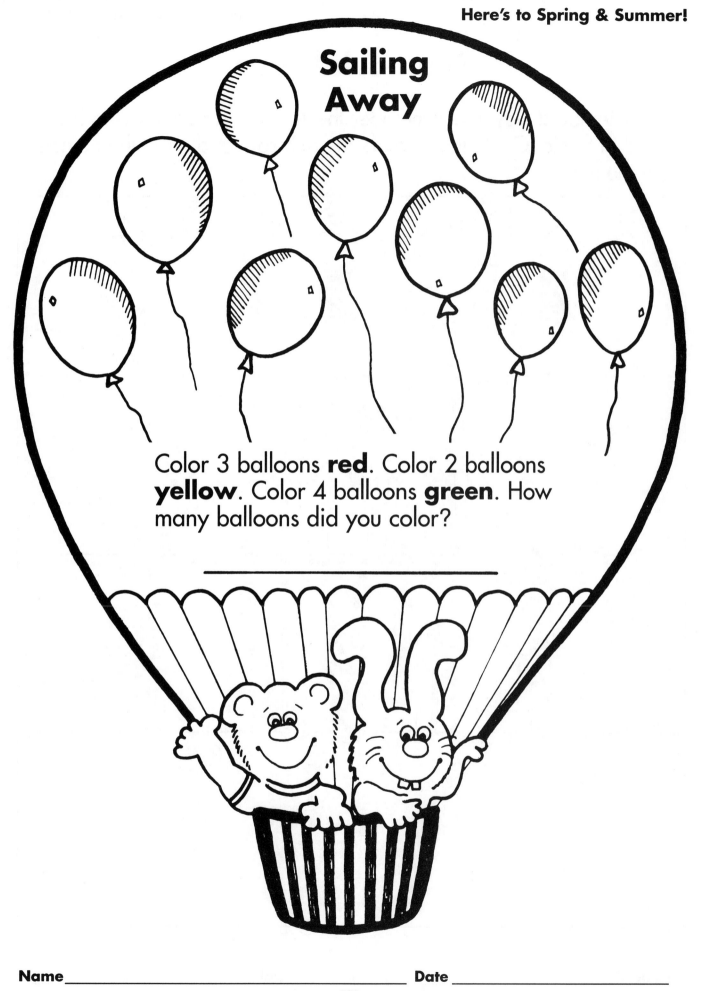

Sailing Away

Color 3 balloons **red**. Color 2 balloons **yellow**. Color 4 balloons **green**. How many balloons did you color?

_____

Memorial Day

On Memorial Day, we remember the American soldiers who have died in battle. Count the soldiers in each row and write the number on the line.

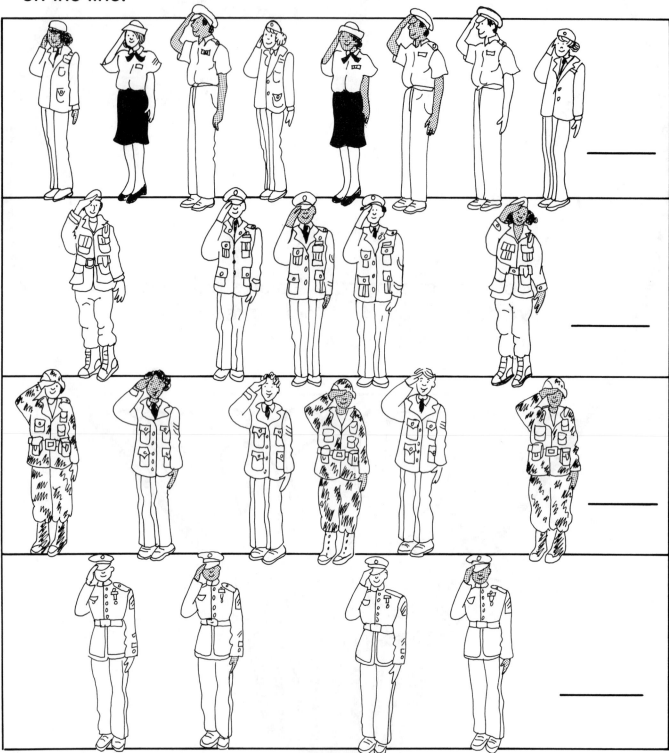

Summer Months

PASTE
HERE

PASTE
HERE

PASTE
HERE

JUNE

JULY

AUGUST

Color, cut
and glue
into the
right box.

Name_____ **Date** _____

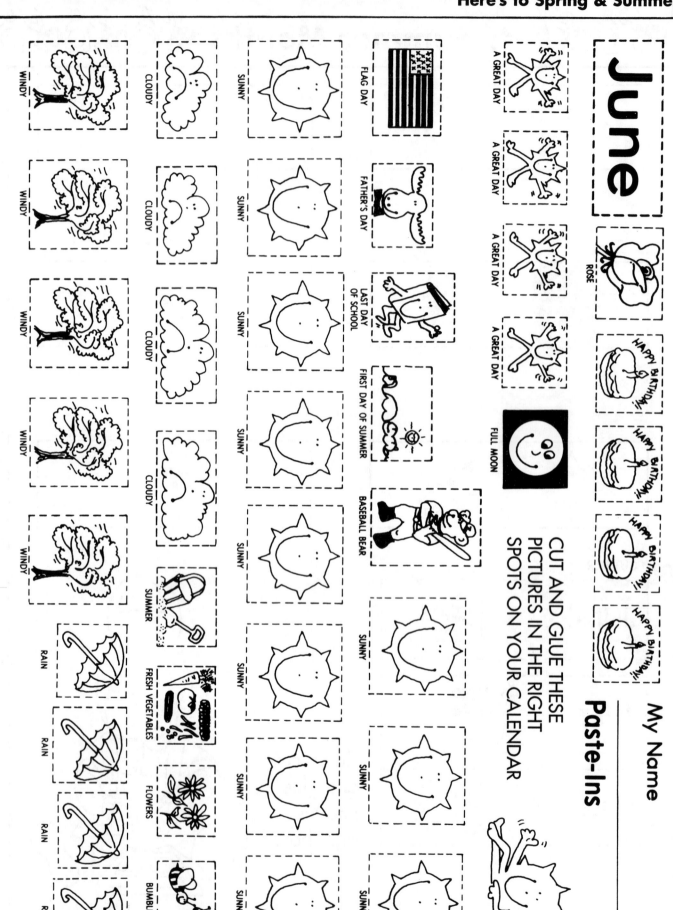

June

My Name

Paste-Ins

CUT AND GLUE THESE
PICTURES IN THE RIGHT
SPOTS ON YOUR CALENDAR

A GREAT DAY

A GREAT DAY

A GREAT DAY

A GREAT DAY

FULL MOON

ROSE

HAPPY BIRTHDAY!

HAPPY BIRTHDAY!

HAPPY BIRTHDAY!

HAPPY BIRTHDAY!

FLAG DAY

FATHER'S DAY

LAST DAY OF SCHOOL

FIRST DAY OF SUMMER

BASEBALL BEAR

SUNNY

SUNNY

SUNNY

SUNNY

SUNNY

SUNNY

SUNNY

SUNNY

SUNNY

SUNNY

CLOUDY

CLOUDY

CLOUDY

CLOUDY

WINDY

WINDY

WINDY

WINDY

WINDY

SUMMER

FRESH VEGETABLES

FLOWERS

BUMBLE BEES

RAIN

RAIN

RAIN

RAIN

 # Fun with Stars & Stripes

Here is what our flag used to look like. At first, it had 13 stars and 13 stripes, because there were 13 states in our country. But as new states joined the country, the flag was changed. Color the flags and count the stars and stripes in each one.

1777
Betsy Ross Flag

How many stars?

_____

How many stripes?

_____

1861

How many stars?

_____

How many stripes?

1795

How many stars?

_____

How many stripes?

_____

1912

How many stars?

_____

How many stripes?

1818

How many stars?

_____

How many stripes?

1960-TODAY

How many stars?

_____

How many stripes?

1818
Great Star Flag

How many stars?

_____

How many stripes?

_____

RED   WHITE   BLUE

Flag Day June 14

Name _____   Date _____

51

Let's Pick Cherries!

Cut out the cherries. Glue them to the cherry tree so that they are in the correct order in each row. Color the cherries red. Yum!

Name_____ **Date** _____

Father's Day Card

Father's Day is the third Sunday in June.
Here is a card you can make.

Cut out on
dotted line.

Color card.
Fold in half.

Love,
MARY

Sign your
name inside!

Name _____ **Date** _____

53

Father's Day Portrait

For Father's Day, draw a picture of yourself for your Dad. Try to draw just your face. Then sign your name at the bottom and write the date. Have fun!

Name_____ **Date** _____

HAPPY FATHER'S DAY!

LOVE,

Cut card along dotted line below.
Color the card and sign your name at the bottom.

Something's Fishy

Carmela and her grandmother are going fishing. When they reach the pond, Carmela is surprised. Something is wrong. Help Carmela find all the "mistakes" in the picture.

Name_____ **Date** _____

First Day of Summer

The first day of summer is usually June 20th, 21st or 22nd. Here is a summer puzzle for you to do. Find each of these 8 words in the puzzle. Look across and down. One is done for you.

X	S	U	M	M	E	R	G
F	B	N	S	W	I	M	S
U	E	F	L	A	G	H	A
V	A	C	A	T	I	O	N
I	C	G	I	E	L	T	D
A	H	B	E	R	S	G	C

HOT
SUMMER
VACATION
FLAG
BEACH
SWIM
WATER
SAND

Name_____   Date _____

57

Summer Fruit Salad

Let's make a fruit salad of summer fruits. Look at the pictures and say the name of the fruit. Write the missing letter on the line.

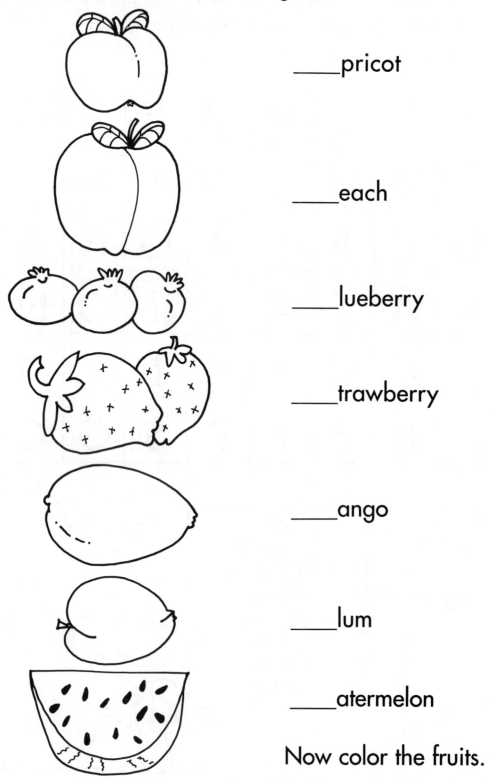

____pricot

____each

____lueberry

____trawberry

____ango

____lum

____atermelon

Now color the fruits.

Name_____ **Date** _____

58

Fishing for Letters

The children want to go fishing. Help them by drawing a fishing line from each fishing pole handle to the fish with the letter that comes next in the alphabet.

Name _____ **Date** _____

Have a Ball!

Help each sports player hit or kick the ball. Color the ball with the highest number.

Name_____ **Date** _____

Ice Cream Sundae

Let's have an ice-cream sundae. Choose toppings that would taste good on a sundae. Draw a line from the topping to the ice cream.

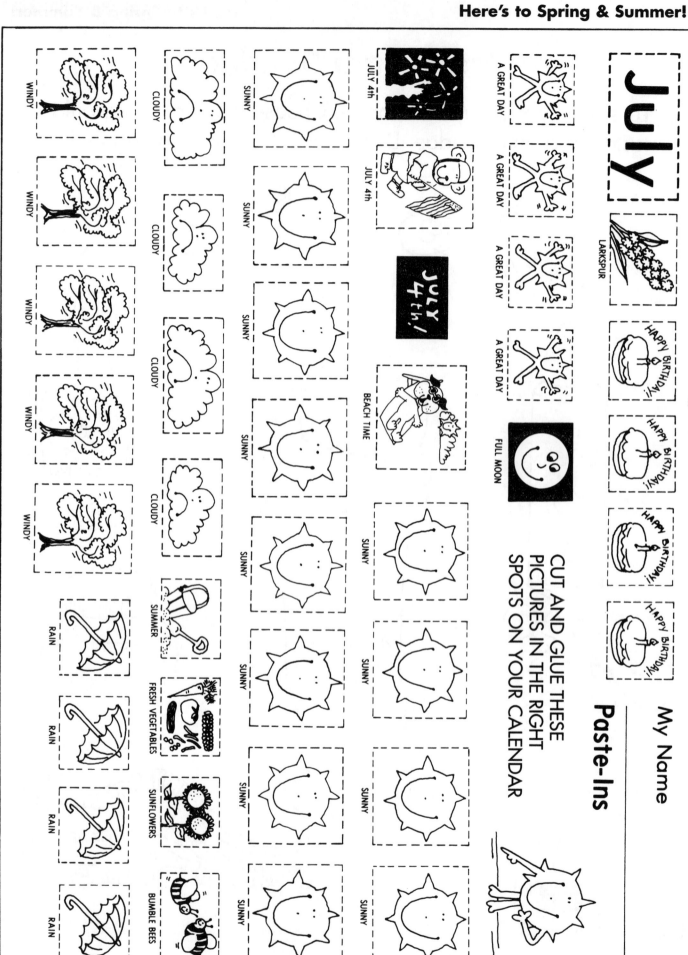

July

My Name

Paste-Ins

CUT AND GLUE THESE
PICTURES IN THE RIGHT
SPOTS ON YOUR CALENDAR

LARKSPUR

HAPPY BIRTHDAY!

A GREAT DAY

FULL MOON

JULY 4th

JULY 4th!

BEACH TIME

SUNNY

WINDY

CLOUDY

RAIN

SUMMER

FRESH VEGETABLES

SUNFLOWERS

BUMBLE BEES

All-American Colors

Color the things that are RED:

apple

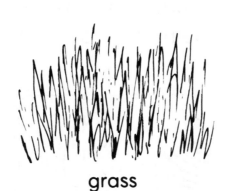

grass

cherries

Color the things that are WHITE:

bananas

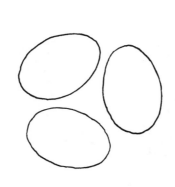

eggs

snowman

Color the things that are BLUE:

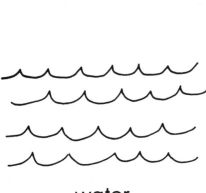

water

blue jay

sun

Name_____   **Date** _____

63

July 4th Count

Below, count the Fourth of July things and write the word for the number on the line.

_____

\- \- \- \- \- \- \- \- \- \- \- \- \- \-

_____

_____

\- \- \- \- \- \- \- \- \- \- \- \- \- \-

_____

_____

\- \- \- \- \- \- \- \- \- \- \- \- \- \-

_____

_____

\- \- \- \- \- \- \- \- \- \- \- \- \- \-

_____

Name_____ **Date** _____

Stars & Stripes

Cut out and glue a *yes* star next to a stripe on the flag if the sentence is true. Cut out and glue a *no* star next to a stripe on the flag if the sentence is not true.

A shoe is a glove.

A child goes to school.

A chair cooks food.

A dog eats a bone.

An adult drives a car.

Yes

Yes

Yes

No

No

No

Name _____ Date _____

65

The First Flag

To make our country's 1st flag, cut out this strip of stars. Count out 13 stars and paste where shown. Color the flag.

BLUE

RED

WHITE

RED

WHITE

RED

WHITE

RED

WHITE

RED

WHITE

RED

Name_____

Date _____

Play Ball

ACROSS:
1. What the pitcher throws.
2. What the runner does to the base.

DOWN:
1. What the batter uses.

It's a Goal!

Find these words. Put a circle around each one. Words can go across or down.

GOAL	FIELD
NET	SCORE
BALL	KICK

A	N	M	G	O	A	L	U	Z	C	F
C	E	Z	U	J	N	J	V	B	D	I
L	T	W	C	K	M	K	I	C	K	E
B	A	L	L	B	O	O	Q	P	M	L
J	S	C	O	R	E	B	T	S	R	D

Name_____ **Date** _____

68

Shell Game

Shells are hidden in this picture. Find and count them.
How many did you find? Put the answer here _____ .
Now color the picture.

Name_____   Date _____

69

August

My Name

Paste-Ins

CUT AND GLUE THESE PICTURES IN THE RIGHT SPOTS ON YOUR CALENDAR

WINDY

WINDY

WINDY

WINDY

WINDY

CLOUDY

CLOUDY

CLOUDY

CLOUDY

CLOUDY

SUNNY

SUNNY

SUNNY

SUNNY

SUNNY

SUNNY

SUNNY

SUNNY

SUNNY

SUNNY

SUNNY

VACATION TIME

BEACH TIME

BEACH TIME

A GREAT DAY

A GREAT DAY

A GREAT DAY

A GREAT DAY

FULL MOON

GLADIOLA

HAPPY BIRTHDAY!

HAPPY BIRTHDAY!

HAPPY BIRTHDAY!

RAIN

RAIN

RAIN

RAIN

SUMMER

FRESH VEGETABLES

SUN FLOWERS

BUMBLE BEES

70

Up, Up...and Away

START

FINISH

BALLOON FIXER

This balloon has a leak. Help the animals find a place to get it fixed.

Name_____ Date_____

71

Who's Who at the Zoo?

Follow the directions near each pair of animals.

Color the monkey on **top** blue.
Color the monkey in the **middle** green.
Color the monkey on the **bottom** brown.

Color the tiger that is **up** orange.
Color the tiger that is **down** black.

Color the elephant on the **left** purple.
Color the elephant on the **right** red.

Color the lion that is **in** yellow.
Color the lion that is **out** pink.

Name_____ Date _____

On a Roll!

Jeremiah loves to skate. But it's hot in the summer! Help him get to the lemonade stand. Color the path with the word that has the same ending sound as the picture.

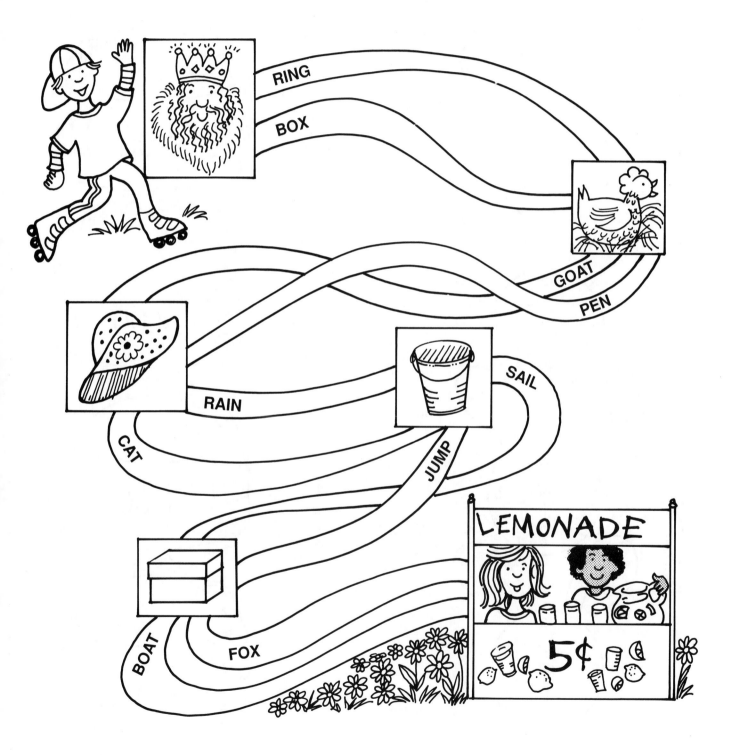

Name_____ Date_____

It's Bunny Time

The bunnies with clocks on their faces can't tell *digital* time. Help them by drawing a line from each bunny to the correct basket.

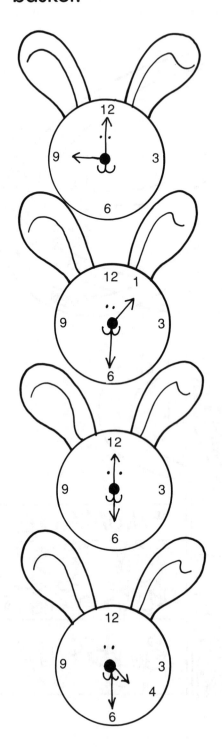

A Fancy Fan

You can make a pretty summer fan. Follow the color code.
Then cut out the fan along the dotted lines. When you fold it
along the solid lines, you will have a fan to help you keep cool!

Color "f" words blue.
Color "l" words green.
Color "m" words red.
Color "n" words yellow.
Color "t" words orange.
Color "s" words purple.

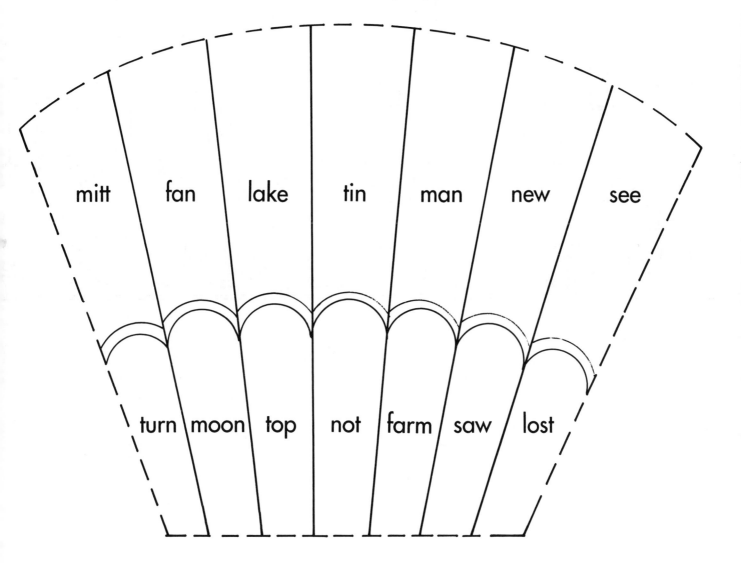

mitt   fan   lake   tin   man   new   see

turn moon top not farm saw lost

Summer in the City

Joycelyn wants to count the "windows" on the city buildings so she can do the addition problems. Will you help her?

4 + 3 = ☐   8 + 2 = ☐

5 + 2 = ☐   3 + 5 = ☐

6 + 4 = ☐   6 + 3 = ☐

Name_____ **Date** _____